I0410358

September 2014

MISSOURI RIVER FLOOD AND DROUGHT

Experts Agree the Corps Took Appropriate Action, Given the Circumstances, but Should Examine New Forecasting Techniques

GAO-14-741

GAO Highlights

Highlights of GAO-14-741, a report to congressional requesters

MISSOURI RIVER FLOOD AND DROUGHT

Experts Agree the Corps Took Appropriate Action, Given the Circumstances, but Should Examine New Forecasting Techniques

Why GAO Did This Study

The Missouri River stretches from western Montana to St. Louis, Missouri. The Corps manages six dams and reservoirs on the river to provide flood control and for other purposes, such as recreation and navigation. The Corps bases reservoir release decisions on the guidance in the Master Manual. In the 2011 flood, the Corps managed the highest runoff volume since 1898, resulting in record reservoir releases. Subsequently, drought occurred in the basin in 2012 and 2013.

GAO was asked to review the Corps' release decisions and communication during the flood and drought. This report examines (1) experts' views on the Corps' release decisions; (2) experts' recommendations to improve the Corps' release decisions; and (3) stakeholders' views on the Corps' communication, as well as any suggested improvements. GAO worked with the National Academy of Sciences to convene a meeting of nine experts to discuss the Corps' data, forecasts, and release decisions. GAO also interviewed 45 Missouri River basin stakeholders, including state and local agencies, among others, to discuss their views on the Corps' communication. The views of stakeholders are not generalizable.

What GAO Recommends

GAO recommends that the Corps evaluate the pros and cons of incorporating new forecasting techniques into its management of the Missouri River reservoirs. The Department of Defense concurred with the recommendation.

View GAO-14-741. For more information, contact Anne-Marie Fennell at (202) 512-3841 or fennella@gao.gov.

What GAO Found

Experts who participated in a GAO-sponsored meeting agreed that the U.S. Army Corps of Engineers (Corps) made appropriate release decisions during the 2011 flood and 2012 and 2013 drought affecting the Missouri River basin, given the severity of these events. These experts acknowledged that the flood was primarily due to extreme rain in eastern Montana in May and June 2011. The experts agreed that no existing forecasting tools could have accurately predicted these extreme rainstorms more than a week in advance. One of the experts also said that the Corps would have needed several months to release enough water from the reservoirs to have sufficient space for the runoff that occurred in 2011, and predicting an extreme runoff year that far in advance is beyond the current state of science. Moreover, the experts agreed that the Corps appropriately followed the drought conservation procedures in the Missouri River Mainstem Reservoir System Master Water Control Manual (Master Manual), which sets out policies for managing the river. The experts agreed that the Corps does not need to change the Master Manual in response to the 2011 flood or subsequent drought. However, some of the experts noted that if the Corps develops improved forecasting tools, it might be useful to evaluate whether changes to the Master Manual would help the Corps to act on information from the new tools.

The experts suggested that improving data systems and introducing new runoff forecasting techniques could improve the Corps' ability to make release decisions in less extreme events than the 2011 flood. These data systems—such as streamgages, weather radar, precipitation gauges, soil moisture monitoring, and monitoring for snow on the plains—are not managed by the Corps, but by other federal and state agencies, which creates challenges beyond the Corps' control. The experts agreed that probabilistic forecasting techniques—which correct for unknown initial conditions using statistical techniques and provide a range of potential outcomes and their likeliness—could help the Corps manage risks better than their current methods that create one forecast estimate. One of the experts said that probabilistic methods could provide greater benefits, such as higher water supply reliability, increased flood protection and hydropower production, and easier implementation of variable flows to create fish and wildlife habitats. Probabilistic techniques are currently used by New York City to support reservoir releases to manage flood risk and meet water quality goals without adding expensive new filtration equipment. Corps officials said that they have not considered using probabilistic techniques in the Missouri River basin because they are not sure the benefits would outweigh the difficulty of creating the models or explaining the new methods to their stakeholders.

During both the flood and drought, the Corps communicated with Missouri River stakeholders in a variety of ways, which most stakeholders GAO spoke with said were effective. Most stakeholders were generally satisfied with the Corps' communication, saying that the information they received from the Corps was timely and sufficient for their purposes. Most stakeholders had at least one suggestion on how the Corps could improve communication; however, there was little consensus on any one suggestion. A few stakeholders suggested that the Corps hold separate conference calls to discuss sensitive response-related issues. Corps officials said that they would consider this in the future.

Contents

Figures

Abbreviations

AHPS	Advanced Hydrologic Prediction Service
cfs	cubic feet per second
CoCoRAHS	Community Collaborative Rain, Hail and Snow Network
Corps	U.S. Army Corps of Engineers
DEP	New York City Department of Environmental Protection
MAF	million acre-feet
Master Manual	Missouri River Mainstem Reservoir System Master Water Control Manual
MRAPS	Missouri River Authorized Purposes Study
NAS	National Academy of Sciences
NOAA	National Oceanic and Atmospheric Administration
NOHRSC	National Operational Hydrologic Remote Sensing Center
NRCS	Natural Resources Conservation Service
NWS	National Weather Service
SCAN	Soil Climate Analysis Network
SNOTEL	snowpack telemetry
USGS	U.S. Geological Survey
WRRDA	Water Resources Reform and Development Act

September 12, 2014

Congressional Requesters

The Missouri River is a critical national resource, stretching 2,341 miles from western Montana to its mouth near St. Louis, Missouri, and flowing through or forming a border for seven states. Between 1933 and 1964, the U.S. Army Corps of Engineers (Corps) built six dams and reservoirs on the mainstem[1] of the Missouri River. The Corps' Missouri River Basin Water Management Division manages these dams and reservoirs for eight authorized purposes: navigation, flood control, irrigation, hydropower, municipal and industrial water supply, water quality, recreation, and fish and wildlife habitat.[2] To manage the river, the Corps uses the Missouri River Mainstem Reservoir System Master Water Control Manual (Master Manual), which was last updated in 2006. The Master Manual describes the river, dams, and reservoirs; identifies key data from other agencies such as the National Oceanic and Atmospheric Administration (NOAA), United States Geological Survey (USGS), and Natural Resources Conservation Service (NRCS); describes the Corps' methods for creating forecasts of the amount of runoff[3] flowing into the reservoirs; and sets out the policies and procedures under which the Corps operates in making decisions about water releases from the dams.

In 2011, large amounts of snow and extreme rains along the Missouri River led to the highest runoff levels since recordkeeping began in 1898 and prompted the Corps to release a record volume of water from the dams to prevent the dams from being overtopped, which could have caused catastrophic dam failure. These high runoff levels and high water

---

[1] The mainstem is the primary downstream segment of a river, as contrasted to its tributaries.

[2] See Flood Control Act of 1944, Pub. L. No. 78-534, § 9, 58 Stat. 887 (1944); H. R. Doc. No. 475, 78th Cong., 2d Sess. 28-29 (1944); S. Doc. No. 191, 78th Cong., 2d Sess. (1944); S. Doc. No. 247, 78th Cong., 2d Sess. 2-5 (1944); *South Dakota v. Ubbelohde*, 330 F.3d 1014, 1019-20 (8th Cir. 2003).

[3] Runoff flows over the land surface, going downhill into rivers and streams. Runoff into the mainstem reservoirs along the Missouri River generally comes from three sources: snowfall in the mountains of Montana and Wyoming; snowfall in plains states, including Montana, North Dakota, South Dakota, and Nebraska; and rainfall throughout the Missouri River basin.

releases caused significant flooding and damage along the river from Montana to Missouri and disruption that affected farms, homes, businesses, industries, public infrastructure, and transportation networks. According to the Corps' After Action Report, the flood costs borne by the Corps were approximately $1 billion, including direct flood damages, response activities during the flood fight, and subsequent repair activities.[4] After the flood, both 2012 and the spring of 2013 were dry, leading to drought conditions in parts of the Missouri River basin and causing the Corps to reduce releases from the dams to conserve water. The Corps' release decisions and communication during the recent flood and drought affected stakeholders with interests in the management of the river—including navigators, municipalities that draw drinking water from the river, farmers who use river water for irrigation, and conservationists seeking to protect fish and bird habitats.

You asked us to review the Corps' release decisions and communication with stakeholders during the 2011 flood and subsequent drought. This report examines (1) experts' views on the Corps' release decisions during the 2011 flood and 2012 and 2013 drought; (2) additional actions, if any, experts recommend to improve the Corps' ability to make future release decisions; and (3) stakeholders' views on how the Corps communicated information during the flood and drought, and improvements, if any, that stakeholders suggest.

To address these objectives, we analyzed documents, consulted with experts, and interviewed stakeholders. Specifically, we reviewed relevant laws and related documents that guide the Corps' release decisions, including the Master Manual. We reviewed documents produced or commissioned by the Corps that describe the details of the Corps' release decisions during the flood and drought. We also reviewed reports by NOAA, the National Weather Service (NWS), USGS, and other agencies describing the recent flood and drought, as well as existing data collection and forecasting systems in the Missouri River basin. In addition, we worked with the National Academy of Sciences to convene a group of nine experts for a 2-day meeting in February 2014. We asked this group of experts to discuss the Corps' data, forecasts, and release decisions during the recent flood and drought (See app. I for a list of the experts

---

[4] Army Corps of Engineers, Northwestern Division, *2011 Missouri River Basin Flood Regional After Action Report*, (Portland, OR: July 2012).

and the questions discussed during the 2-day meeting). Finally, using a standard set of questions, we interviewed 45 stakeholders from the Missouri River basin, selected to represent organizations from each of the seven states (Iowa, Kansas, Missouri, Montana, Nebraska, North Dakota, and South Dakota) and each of the eight authorized purposes. These stakeholders included city government officials from communities along the river, officials from state emergency management agencies, state fish and wildlife agencies, and individuals representing companies in the navigation industry. These stakeholder interviews provide key insights and illustrate opinions concerning Missouri River basin issues, however the results of our interviews cannot be used to make generalizations about all views. A more detailed description of our objectives, scope, and methodology is presented in appendix II. We conducted this performance audit from August 2012 to September 2014 in accordance with generally accepted government auditing standards. Those standards require that we plan and perform the audit to obtain sufficient, appropriate evidence to provide a reasonable basis for our findings and conclusions based on our audit objectives. We believe that the evidence obtained provides a reasonable basis for our findings and conclusions based on our audit objectives.

Background

Missouri River Basin and the Mainstem Dams

The Missouri River basin extends from the Rocky Mountains across portions of the Midwest and Great Plains, covering roughly one-sixth of the continental United States (see fig. 1).

Figure 1: Missouri River Basin and the Six Mainstem Dams and Reservoirs

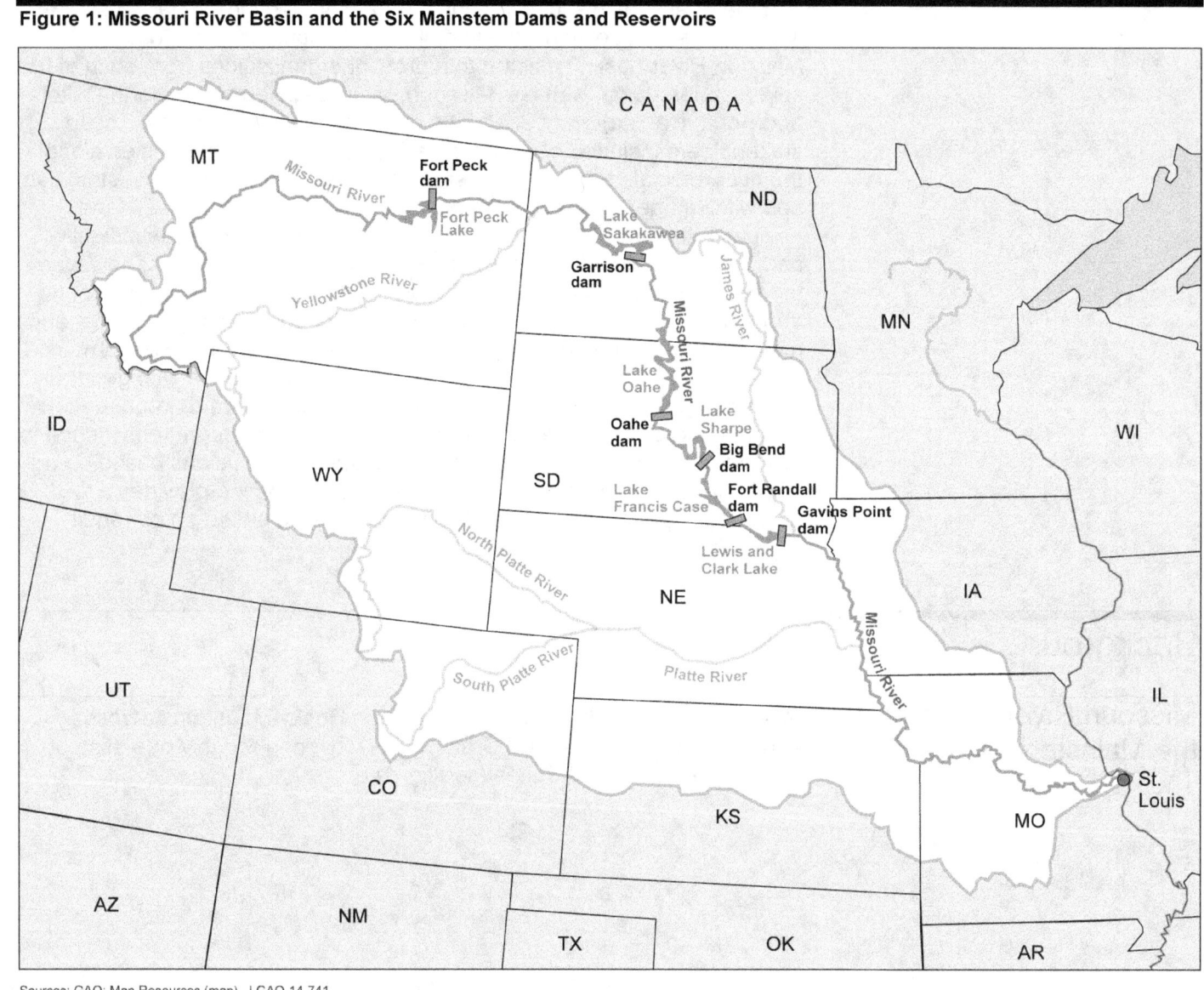

Sources: GAO; Map Resources (map). | GAO-14-741

Of the six dams along the mainstem of the Missouri River, one is in Montana (Fort Peck), one is in North Dakota (Garrison), three are in South Dakota (Oahe, Big Bend, and Fort Randall), and one is along the South Dakota-Nebraska border (Gavins Point). This reservoir system is the largest in the United States and contains about 73.1 million acre-feet (MAF) of water storage capacity. A majority of the system's storage capacity is in the three upstream reservoirs—Fort Peck Lake, Lake Sakakawea, and Lake Oahe. Gavins Point dam is the furthest downstream of the six dams, and its water releases support all uses of the river below the reservoir system. Gavins Point dam is about 811 miles upstream from the mouth of the Missouri, where it enters the Mississippi River near St. Louis; water released from Gavins Point dam takes about 10 days to reach the Mississippi River.

The Master Manual and Authorized Purposes

The Master Manual lays out procedures for the Corps' management of the six Missouri River mainstem dams as a system. In the Master Manual, the Corps attempts to balance the eight congressionally authorized purposes of the river.[5] The current Master Manual was developed over the course of 17 years and involved extensive consultation between the Corps and basin stakeholders, as well as multiple lawsuits.[6] Key changes

---

[5] A 2004 federal district court decision, *In re Operation of the Missouri. River Sys. Litig.* 363 F. Supp. 2d 1145 (D. Minn., 2004), noted that while courts acknowledge that the dominant functions of the Flood Control Act of 1944 include flood control and downstream navigation, they also acknowledge that other river interests should be provided for. The district court cited a 2003 appellate court decision (*South Dakota v. Ubbelohde*, 330 F.3d 1014, 1027(8th Cir. 2003)) acknowledging that the Flood Control Act requires that "the Corps must strike a balance among many interests, including flood control, navigation, and recreation." The district court additionally noted that the language of the Flood Control Act does not require a particular outcome, but rather that the Corps consider all interests in its operations. *Missouri River*, 363 F. Supp. 2d at 1153.

[6] In response to the Corps' issuance of a revised Master Manual in March 2004, multiple parties filed lawsuits in various federal district courts seeking to protect their river interests. This multidistrict litigation was consolidated into one case. The June 2004 district court decision in this consolidated case, *In re Operation of the Mo. River Sys., Litig.* 363 F. Supp. 2d 1145 (D. Minn., 2004), among other things, found that the Corps' prioritization of river interests is discretionary and granted the Corps' Motion for Summary Judgment on Flood Control Act claims holding that the Corps' "2004 Master Manual complies with the [Flood Control Act]." This aspect of the district court decision was affirmed on appeal in 2005. *Am. Rivers, Inc. v. United States Army Corps of Eng'rs.*, 421 F. 3d 618 (8th Cir. 2005). The appellate court affirmed that the "Corps' balancing of water-use interests in the 2004 Master Manual is in accordance with the [Flood Control Act]." Id. at 630.

in the Master Manual revision include more rapid measures taken in response to drought conditions, changes in the water levels in the upper three reservoirs during the spring to support fish spawning, and measures to support endangered species along the river.

The Master Manual allocates water within the reservoir system to four different storage zones (see fig. 2):

- The Permanent Pool includes about 25 percent of the system's storage capacity and is intended to be full at all times to maintain a minimum amount of water in the reservoirs for hydropower production, fish and wildlife in and along the reservoirs, and reservoir-based recreation.

- The Carryover Multiple Use Zone stores water for irrigation, navigation, hydropower, water supply, recreation, water quality control, and fish and wildlife. This zone is intended to maintain downstream river flows, although at lower levels, even in a succession of dry years. When the basin is not experiencing a drought, this zone is designed to be full when the runoff year begins on March 1. During times of drought, water from this zone is used to support the aforementioned authorized purposes, though at lower levels.

- The Annual Flood Control and Multiple Use Zone provides storage space for spring and summer runoff that can be used throughout the year to support all authorized purposes. The Master Manual sets a goal of having this zone empty on or about March 1 of every year, so any water that is stored here during the spring and summer is meant to be released prior to the start of the next runoff season, which is approximately March 1.

- The Exclusive Flood Control Zone is only used to store floodwaters in extreme and unpredictable floods and is emptied as rapidly as downstream conditions permit.

Figure 2: Missouri River Reservoir System Storage Zones

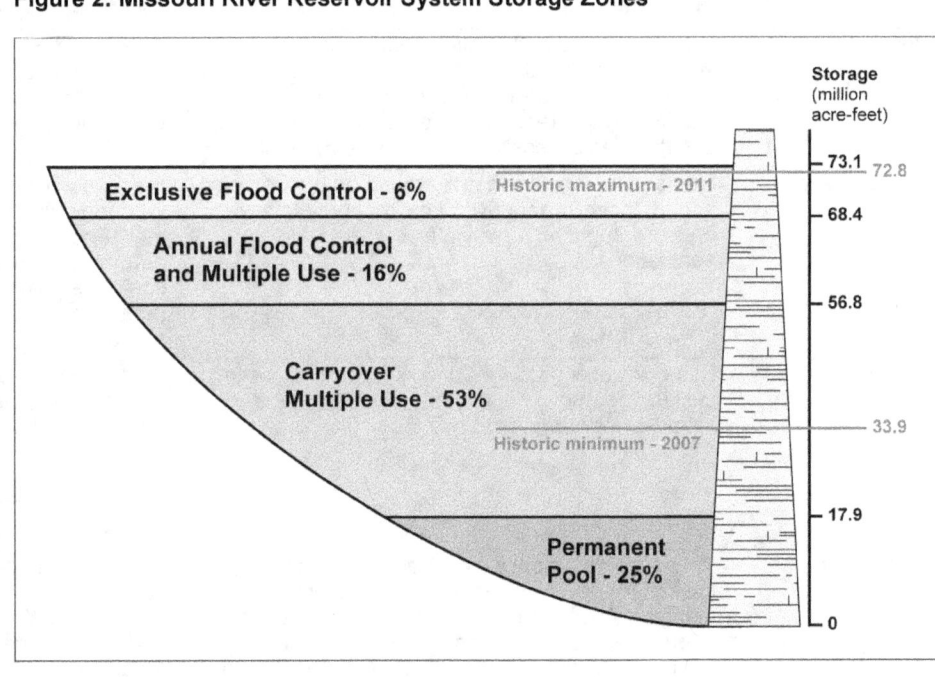

Source: U.S. Army Corps of Engineers. | GAO-14-741

Note: Percentages refer to a storage zone's percent of the total storage in the Missouri River Reservoir System.

The eight authorized purposes of the system have different water needs, and the Master Manual addresses each of these purposes (see table 1).

Table 1: Missouri River Authorized Purposes and Key Master Manual Provisions

Authorized purpose	Description	Key Master Manual provisions
Flood control	Requires empty space in the reservoirs. Water is captured during high runoff events in the spring and summer and released through the remainder of the year.	Targets March 1 reservoir level to be 56.8 million acre-feet (MAF) each year. This target results in 16.3 MAF of storage space for spring and summer runoff; which was based on historic records. The U.S. Army Corps of Engineers (Corps) has flexibility during a flood to respond to rapidly changing conditions and make release decisions to protect dam infrastructure.
Navigation	Navigation channel from Sioux City, Iowa, to St. Louis, Missouri, is supported by flows from the reservoir system. A normal 8-month navigation season lasts from April to December.	The volume of water stored in the reservoir system on March 15 determines the navigation channel depth for the first half of the navigation season. Storage levels on July 1 determine the navigation channel depth for the second half of the season, as well as the total length of the season.[a]

Authorized purpose	Description	Key Master Manual provisions
Recreation	Includes fishing and boating on the reservoirs and in the river below the reservoir system. Recreation on the three upstream reservoirs is adversely affected by low reservoir levels during drought due to difficulties accessing the reservoir via boat.	To support fishing as a recreational activity in the three upper reservoirs, the Corps attempts to provide rising reservoirs in the spring to support habitat for reservoir fish spawning.
Fish and wildlife	Fish and wildlife live in and around both reservoirs and the downstream river. Low reservoir levels during drought adversely affect reservoir fish populations.	Relatively uniform release rates during spawning season for certain fish species is beneficial, and attempts are made, considering requirements for other authorized purposes, to minimize release fluctuations during these times. As noted above, the Corps attempts to provide rising reservoirs in the spring to support habitat for reservoir fish spawning.
Hydropower	Hydropower is produced at all six of the dams in the system. The power is marketed by the Western Area Power Administration.	To the extent possible, all water releases are passed through the generating units to produce power. The Corps determines the total amount of water released through the dams daily (and thus the amount of power to be produced). Within the daily total and other constraints, the Western Area Power Administration has flexibility to manage releases on a real-time basis to meet power demand.
Municipal and industrial water supply	There are municipal water intakes, as well as intakes for power plants at numerous locations along the Missouri River. Ninety-four percent of the population served by these intakes is located below the reservoir system. Similarly, 75 percent of the generating capacity along the river comes from power plants with intakes below the reservoir system.	During the April-to-December navigation season, navigation flows are generally sufficient to ensure supply to municipal and industrial water intakes. The release rate during the winter is set based on volume of water in the reservoir system on September 1. During the winter, the Corps has the flexibility to increase releases to help ensure continued access by these intakes, though ultimate responsibility for maintaining access to the river lies with the intake owners.
Water quality	Water quality characteristics that are of greatest concern in the basin are chemical constituents, which affect human health, plant and animal life, and the uses of the water such as irrigation; temperatures, which affect fisheries and the aquatic environment; biological organisms, which affect human health; and taste, odor, and floating materials, which affect the water's potability.	Generally, release levels sufficient to support municipal and industrial water supply are sufficient to meet water quality requirements.
Irrigation	Federally developed irrigation projects to be supplied directly from the system were envisioned, but there currently is little significant federal irrigation development in the system. However, water from the reservoir and the river is used by private irrigators.	Generally, release levels sufficient to support other authorized purposes are sufficient to meet irrigation requirements.

Source: GAO analysis of information from the Corps. | GAO-14-741

[a]More specifically, the volume of water in the reservoir system on March 15 determines the "service level" that will be provided to navigation. The service level dictates downstream flow targets—for example, a certain volume of water through a particular stretch of river. These flow targets are related to channel depth.

In addition, some of the Corps' reservoir management is related to compliance with the Endangered Species Act of 1973, as amended.[7] Two bird species nest along the river from May to August: the endangered least tern and threatened piping plover. Releases from Gavins Point, Fort Randall, and Garrison dams have been modified to accommodate these bird species by adapting releases to prevent, as much as possible, inundation of bird nests along the river.[8] In addition, one endangered fish species, the pallid sturgeon, lives in the Missouri River. For the pallid sturgeon, the Master Manual calls for two "pulses" of water (temporary higher releases) from Gavins Point dam in the spring to mimic the higher spring river flows that occurred prior to the construction of the mainstem reservoirs. The last spring pulse was implemented in 2009; pulses were cancelled in 2010 and 2011 due to high water levels downstream. According to Corps officials, a 2011 independent review panel questioned the efficacy of the spring pulse and the Fish and Wildlife Service and the Corps are, therefore, currently reevaluating the pulse.

Hydrologic Data and Forecasting for Reservoir Management

The Corps uses numerous types of hydrologic data—data relating to the movement and distribution of water in the basin—to track current conditions in the basin. Most of these data are collected by other federal agencies as part of nationwide efforts to gather weather and hydrologic data (see table 2).

---

[7] Pub. L. No. 93-205, 87 Stat. 884 (1973) (codified as amended at 16 U.S.C. §§ 1531-44).

[8] At Gavins Point, this is done by raising releases in May, when the birds begin nesting, to the levels that will likely be needed to support downstream purposes in July and August. This prevents birds from nesting too close to the river and being inundated by higher late-summer flows. At Fort Randall and Garrison dams, releases are managed to provide consistent peak river levels below the dams.

Table 2: Selected Hydrologic Data Used by the U.S. Army Corps of Engineers to Manage the Missouri River Reservoirs

Type of data	Agency	Program description	Types of data used by the Corps	Status of data collection within the Upper Missouri River basin
Streamflow	United States Geological Survey (USGS)	The National Streamflow Information Program collects streamflow data through its national streamgage network,[a] which continuously measures the level and flow of rivers and streams at 8,025 active continuous streamgages nationwide for distribution on the Internet.	Streamgages can provide information on streamflow as a discharge measurement (the amount of water moving through the river, for example, measured in cubic feet per second) or as a river stage measurement (the current height of the water in the river in feet).	As of May 2014, there were 892 streamgages.
Mountain snowpack	Natural Resources Conservation Service (NRCS)	NRCS operates 885 Snow Telemetry (SNOTEL) sites in the western United States, which transmit snow depth and climate parameters in near real time. In addition, the NRCS snow course network conducts manual surveys of snow depth at about 956 sites in the United States.	Both SNOTEL sites and snow courses gather information about snow depth as well as the snow-water equivalent, which is the amount of water in the snowpack.	As of May 2014, there were 135 active SNOTEL sites. During the winter of 2013-2014, NRCS conducted 426 manual snow surveys at no less than 113 sites.
Plains snowpack	National Oceanic and Atmospheric Administration (NOAA)[b]	The National Operational Hydrologic Remote Sensing Center (NOHRSC) produces a map of snow conditions in the United States daily based on a combination of airborne surveys, satellite observations, and on-the-ground field measurements.[c]	NOHRSC produces products, such as maps, of modeled snow-water equivalent across 31 states and 8 Canadian provinces. NOHRSC also provides information about soil moisture based on their airborne surveys.	As of 2013, there were 167 flight lines along which airborne surveys were taken.
Precipitation	National Weather Service (NWS)	NWS collects snow and rain data in the continental United States with 143 weather radars and 10,000 precipitation gauges. Many of these gauges are owned and operated by other federal agencies; state, municipal, and tribal governments; and citizen observers.[d]	Radar-detected precipitation and on-the-ground precipitation amounts from rain gauges are combined and analyzed to provide estimates of precipitation.	Radar coverage and precipitation gauges are sparse in the Upper Missouri River basin.
Soil moisture[e]	NRCS	Through the Soil Climate Analysis Network (SCAN), NRCS collects information on climate and soil.	Soil moisture as well as soil temperature, air temperature, air pressure, and other measures.	As of June 2014, there were 10 SCAN sites: 8 in Montana, and 1 each in North Dakota and South Dakota.

Source: GAO analysis of agency documents. | GAO-14-741

[a]USGS's National Streamflow Information Program defines a "streamgage" as an active, continuously functioning device placed in a river or stream to measure water levels to aid in the estimation of mean daily streamflow throughout the year.

[b]In addition to federal efforts to collect plains snowpack data, some states have their own programs. For example, the North Dakota State Water Commission's Atmospheric Resource Board Cooperative Observer Network collects data on daily snowfall, monthly snowpack, and snow-water equivalent through a network of volunteer observers in North Dakota.

[c]The Corps manages a cooperative snow survey program that collects on-the-ground measurements of plains snowpack and snow-water equivalent at approximately 25 locations in the Missouri River basin, including near several of the reservoirs. The Corps provides information from these snow surveys to NOHRSC to help verify and validate the NOHRSC models.

[d]In addition, the Community Collaborative Rain, Hail and Snow Network also collects precipitation data through a community-based network of volunteers.

[e]The High Plains Regional Climate Center manages an Automated Weather Data Network that collects air temperature, precipitation, soil temperature, wind speed, and other measures. A few stations in this network collect information about soil moisture, including approximately 30 stations in the Missouri River basin, mostly in Nebraska and South Dakota.

Reports by federal agencies and others have highlighted limitations in some of these data collection efforts in the Missouri River basin.

- **Streamflow.** According to USGS data and an October 2012 report by the Corps assessing post-flood vulnerabilities, loss of streamgages in the basin has reduced available information about streamflows.[9] For example, according to USGS data, operation of 79 streamgages in the Missouri River basin has been discontinued in the last 10 years; this represents about 9 percent of the streamgages in the basin.

- **Soil Moisture.** The October 2012 Corps' vulnerability report and a December 2011 Independent Technical Review Panel commissioned by the Corps indicate that data on soil moisture in the Missouri River basin is currently limited.[10] The October 2012 Corps' vulnerability report recommended that soil moisture be measured at predefined locations in plains states. Data on soil moisture can indicate how much of the precipitation that falls can be expected to run off into the reservoir system. For example, if soils are dry then precipitation is more likely to soak into the soil than to runoff into nearby rivers or streams.

- **Plains snowpack.** Three reports have recently identified limitations in plains snowpack data: the October 2012 Corps' vulnerability report, the December 2011 Independent Technical Review Panel Report, and

---

[9] U.S. Army Corps of Engineers, Northwestern Division, *Missouri River Flood 2011 Vulnerabilities Assessment Report: Volume II Technical Report* (October 2012).

[10] Independent Technical Review Panel, *Review of the Regulation of the Missouri River Mainstem Reservoir System During the Flood of 2011*, (December 2011).

a May 2012 assessment of forecasting during the Missouri River flood by the NWS.[11] For example, the May 2012 NWS report noted that the National Operational Hydrologic Remote Sensing Center (NOHRSC) provides modeled information on snow-water equivalent, but that observational data in the basin are sparse and not always representative of basin-wide conditions.

- **Precipitation.** The May 2012 assessment of NWS forecasting also noted that precipitation gauge and radar data on precipitation in the Missouri River basin were insufficient during the flood.

Agencies have begun taking steps to address some data limitations. For example, in response to the December 2011 Independent Technical Review Panel Report, the Corps worked with officials from NOAA and NRCS, among others, to develop an interagency proposal, released in February 2013, to create a snowpack and soil moisture monitoring system in the plains.[12] Under the proposal, the agencies would (1) enhance existing climate stations with snow depth and soil moisture sensors; (2) install new climate stations in the basin to enhance existing coverage; (3) enhance NOHRSC airborne surveys; (4) identify and train volunteer or part-time hires to conduct manual snow sampling; and (5) fund state coordinator positions in Montana, Nebraska, North Dakota, South Dakota, and Wyoming to coordinate snow surveys and other snow data networks at a state level. The Water Resources Reform and Development Act (WRRDA) of 2014, enacted into law in June 2014, included a requirement that the Secretary of the Army, in coordination with other specified agencies, develop this type of monitoring system in the Upper Missouri River Basin.[13] In addition, NWS has developed a new technology, the Multi-Radar Multi-Sensor system, which integrates information from NWS, Canadian, and other radar systems with on-the-ground precipitation gauge information and model data to provide better estimates of precipitation. According to NWS officials, the Multi-Radar Multi-Sensor system is also capable of mitigating some gaps in radar coverage by extending the effective range of radar-based precipitation

---

[11] National Oceanic and Atmospheric Administration, National Weather Service, *Service Assessment: The Missouri/Souris River Floods of May – August 2011*, (May 2012).

[12] Upper Missouri River Basin Monitoring Committee, *Snow Sampling and Instrumentation Recommendations* (Feb. 1, 2013).

[13] Pub. L. No. 113-121, § 4003, 128 Stat. 1193 (2014).

estimates from individual radars. According to NWS officials, this technology will be implemented nationwide by the end of 2014.

According to Corps documents and officials, the Corps uses hydrologic data as an input to forecasts used to manage the reservoir system. The Corps runs two key forecasts to generate information for basin stakeholders and to make reservoir release decisions.

- **Monthly forecast.** On a monthly basis, or more frequently as needed, the Corps produces a forecast of the expected annual runoff for the remainder of the calendar year. This forecast takes into consideration current basin conditions, such as soil moisture and snowpack, as well as long-range weather outlooks and historical trends. The Corps produces a "basic" forecast, and then adjusts that forecast by a predetermined percentage to generate "upper basic" and "lower basic" forecasts to create a range of potential runoff conditions. According to Corps officials, the upper and lower basic forecasts are designed to be approximately one standard deviation away from the basic forecast and cover approximately 80 percent of the likely variation in expected runoff based on an analysis of historic runoff records. Each month, these runoff forecast estimates are used as input to the 3-week forecast, which forecasts reservoir inflows, releases, storage levels, and hydropower generation, among other things. According to Corps officials, this forecast is used by basin stakeholders to make business decisions that are affected by reservoir releases. For example, the Western Area Power Administration, which is responsible for marketing all the hydropower generated by the six dams, makes power purchase decisions based on this forecast. In addition, the Corps makes some reservoir release decisions based on the monthly forecast, particularly to move water between the six reservoirs to adjust to current weather conditions or support downstream uses.

- **Three-week forecast.** On a weekly basis, or more frequently as needed, the Corps produces a forecast of reservoir inflows, outflows, storage, and power generation over the next 3-to-5 weeks. According to Corps officials, this model uses "water on the ground" information—specifically streamflows and reservoir levels—combined with information from the basic monthly forecast. Officials said this is the primary model they use to set daily and weekly reservoir releases and that they try not to deviate significantly from projected releases at Fort Peck and Garrison dams in this forecast, unless there are unusual circumstances. Adjustments at the other four dams are routinely made to respond to changing conditions on the ground, such as rainfall below the reservoir system.

The Corps' current runoff forecasts are deterministic, meaning that the models create a single forecast based on the existing hydrologic data. Although the monthly runoff forecast also includes the upper basic and lower basic conditions, these are still deterministic because they are generated by using a multiple of the basic forecast. However, according to NOAA documents, error can be introduced into deterministic forecasts when initial hydrologic conditions are not fully known. According to NWS officials, a different type of forecasting—called probabilistic forecasting—attempts to account for uncertainty in the forecast by, for example, using statistical techniques to simulate multiple, slightly different initial conditions. These officials said that probabilistic forecasts provide a range of potential outcomes and their likeliness. Probabilistic techniques are used extensively in weather forecasting both for routine forecasts and for more rare events such as hurricanes, according to NWS officials.

The 2011 Flood and 2012 and 2013 Drought

Annual runoff into the Missouri River reservoir system can vary significantly from year to year (see fig. 3). The lowest runoff year was 1931, with 10.6 MAF of runoff. The highest runoff year was in 2011, with 61 MAF; 61 MAF is about enough water to cover nearly the entire state of Oregon (61.4 million acres) in water 1 foot-deep. Prior to 2011, the highest runoff, which also caused flooding along the river, was 49 MAF in 1997. Runoff in 2011 was about 25 percent greater than in 1997 and 148 percent greater than the historical median of 24.6 MAF.[14]

---

[14] Since the historical median runoff for the Missouri River is 24.6 MAF, half the years had runoff greater than 24.6 MAF, and half the years had runoff less than 24.6 MAF.

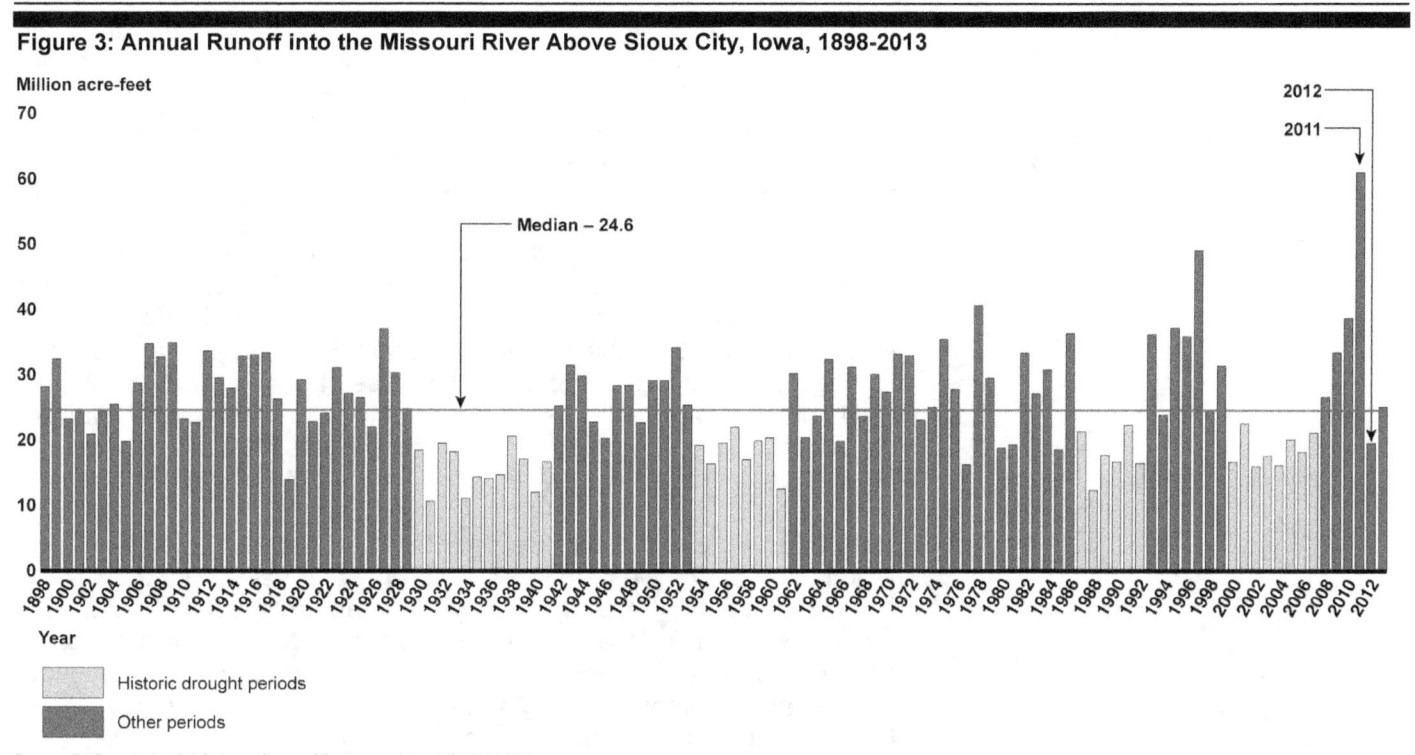

Figure 3: Annual Runoff into the Missouri River Above Sioux City, Iowa, 1898-2013

Source: GAO analysis of U.S. Army Corps of Engineers data. | GAO-14-741

According to the May 2012 assessment of NWS forecasting, several factors combined in 2011 to produce record runoff: wet soil conditions throughout the basin leading into the winter of 2010-2011, high snowpack in both the plains and mountains, and extreme rainfall in May and June of 2011.

- **Wet basin conditions.** After experiencing a drought between 2000 and 2008, the Missouri River basin experienced relatively wet years in both 2009 and 2010. According to a December 2013 NOAA report examining climate extremes in the Missouri River basin, 2010 was the fifth wettest year on record.[15] This precipitation created wet soil moisture conditions throughout the upper basin in the fall of 2010.

---

[15] National Oceanic and Atmospheric Administration, *CLIMATE ASSESSMENT REPORT: Understanding and Explaining Climate Extremes in the Missouri River Basin Associated with the 2011 Flooding* (Boulder, CO: Dec. 27, 2013).

- **Plains snowpack.** Snow can accumulate on the plains through late March or early April. In 2011, total snowfall in the Missouri River basin plains states was well above average, and the snowpack was greater than usual. Numerous cities in the basin set new seasonal snowfall records. For example, Williston, North Dakota, had 107 inches of snow, compared with a long-term average of about 35 inches.

- **Mountain snowpack.** Snowpack generally accumulates in the mountains of Montana and Wyoming throughout the winter, peaking in mid-April and then providing runoff as it melts through May and June. As of March 1, 2011, the mountain snowpack was slightly above average at about 110 percent of normal (see fig. 4). However, late April and May were extremely wet and cold, and mountain snowpack continued to build to record levels in many areas. Mountain snowpack in 2011 peaked in early May at approximately 140 percent of normal.

- **Rainfall in May and June.** Record rain fell in Montana, northern Wyoming, and the western Dakotas in May and early June 2011. Areas of south central and southeast Montana received as much as 15 inches of rain in May, which is 12 inches above normal. Most of eastern Montana received at least three times more precipitation than normal, and the month of May and was ranked as one of the wettest Mays on record in Montana, Wyoming, North Dakota, South Dakota, and Nebraska. Rain continued to fall in June, with Montana, North Dakota, South Dakota, and Nebraska receiving 3 to 8 inches more rain than normal.

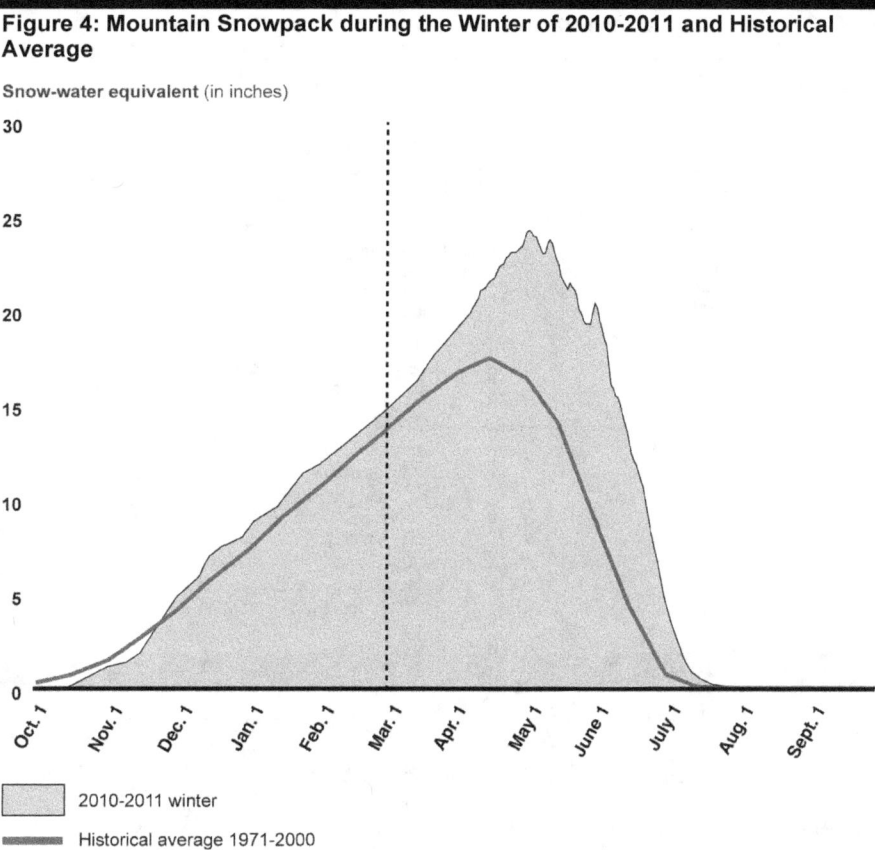

Figure 4: Mountain Snowpack during the Winter of 2010-2011 and Historical Average

Snow-water equivalent (in inches)

- 2010-2011 winter
- Historical average 1971-2000
- Start of the runoff season

Source: U.S. Army Corps of Engineers. | GAO-14-741

As these weather conditions unfolded in 2011, the Corps continued to modify its release rates from the reservoir system (see fig. 5). In early April, the Corps began flood control operations by increasing releases from Gavins Point in response to the above average mountain snowpack. The Corps continued increasing releases throughout April and May, reaching 50,000 cubic feet per second (cfs) on May 9 and surpassing the previous high release rate of 70,000 cfs (set in 1997) on May 29. Release rates increased particularly fast between late May and late June, when releases peaked at about 160,000 cfs, more than double the previous high release rate; 160,000 cfs is about the amount of water from two Olympic-sized swimming pools going past a single point in 1 second. Gavins Point release rates remained above 100,000 cfs until August 31, and it was not until December that releases returned to a more normal rate of 35,000 cfs.

GAO-14-741 Missouri River Flood and Drought

Figure 5: Gavins Point Release Rate and Key Events during 2011 Flood

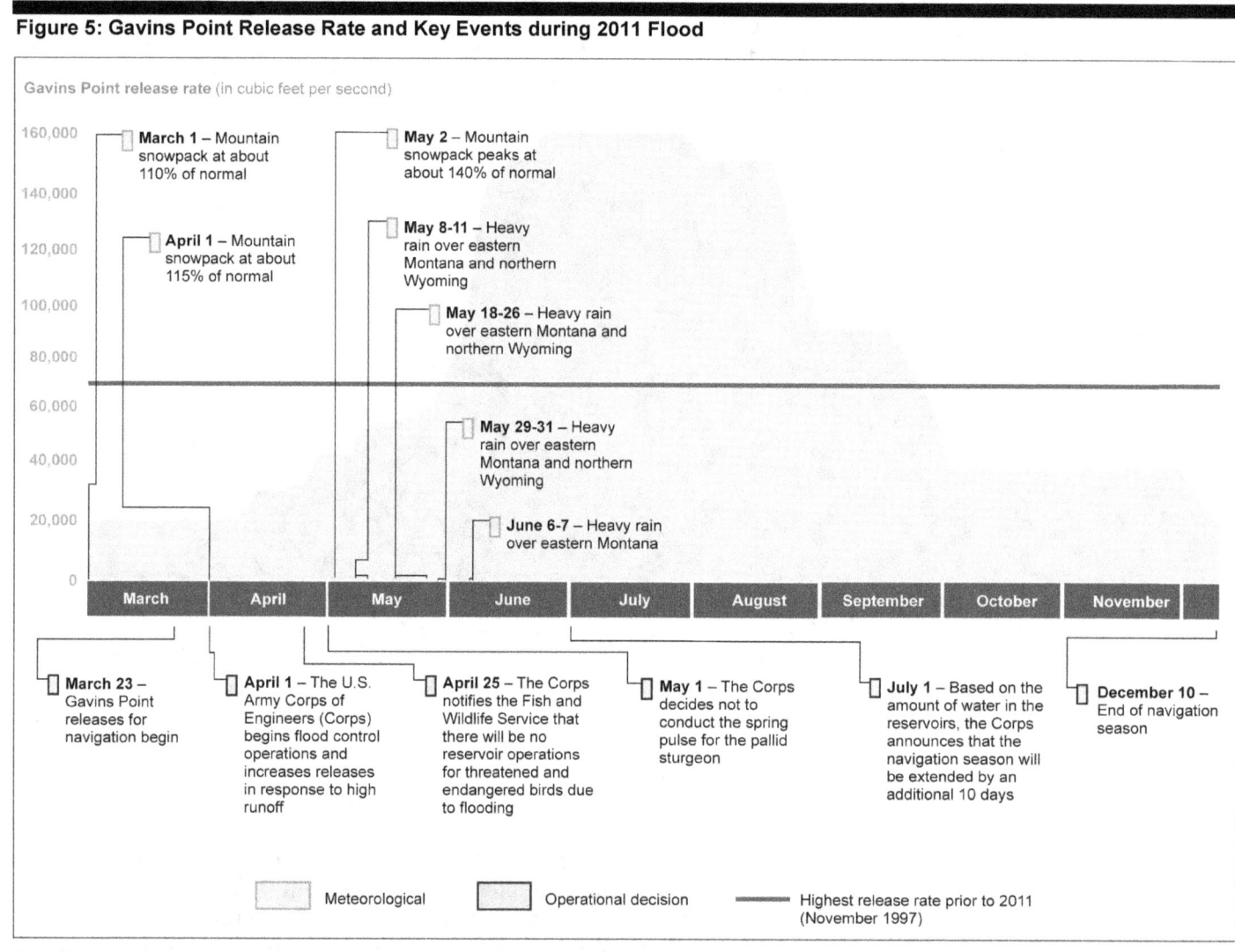

Source: GAO analysis of Corps data. | GAO-14-741

In the fall of 2011, as basin stakeholders and the Corps were repairing infrastructure and recovering from the flood, there was concern that additional flooding would occur in 2012. However, 2012 brought drought throughout the Missouri River basin. Nebraska and Wyoming experienced their driest year in 118 years of recordkeeping, and several other states in the basin also had very dry years. For example, Missouri had its seventh driest year, Iowa had its 11th driest year, and South Dakota had its 13th driest year.

Drought intensity, as defined by the U.S. Drought Monitor, increased from January through July of 2012, at which point moderate and severe drought conditions were present in southern Montana, western South Dakota, western Nebraska, and Wyoming.[16] Conditions worsened during the summer, and by October 2012, extreme and exceptional drought conditions were present across Wyoming, South Dakota, Nebraska, and western Iowa. Total runoff into the Missouri River mainstem reservoir system in 2012 was 19.5 MAF, or about 77 percent of normal runoff. In addition, runoff into the Missouri River below the reservoir system was also extremely low at 51 percent of normal runoff.

As drought conditions evolved in 2012, the Corps made release decisions based on guidelines in the Master Manual, exercising flexibility in certain circumstances. For example, navigation releases are to be based on the volume of water in the reservoirs on March 15 (for April to July releases) and July 1 (for August to December releases).[17] In 2012, the reservoirs were sufficiently full on March 15 to support full-service to navigation, meaning flows high enough for a 9-foot deep channel. On July 1, there was a sufficient volume of water in the reservoirs for the Master Manual to call for a full-length navigation season, which the Corps executed. According to a Corps report describing its management of the reservoir system in 2012, severe drought in the lower basin during the summer required higher-than-normal releases from Gavins Point to maintain the navigation flows called for in the Master Manual.[18] Similarly, winter releases are to be based on the volume of water in the reservoir system on September 1.[19] In 2012, the reservoirs were depleted by the drought,

---

[16] The U.S. Drought Monitor is a joint program operated by NOAA, the U.S. Department of Agriculture, and the University of Nebraska – Lincoln. The U.S. Drought Monitor produces a weekly map of drought conditions around the country, based on measurements of climatic, hydrologic, and soil conditions, as well as reported impacts and observations from more than 350 contributors.

[17] According to the Master Manual, March 15 reservoir levels must be at least 54.5 MAF to initiate full-service to navigation. July 1 reservoir levels must be at least 57 MAF to continue full-service to navigation for the remainder of the season.

[18] U.S. Army Corps of Engineers, Northwestern Division, *Missouri River Mainstem Reservoir System: Summary of Actual 2012 Regulation* (Omaha, NE: June 2013).

[19] According to the Master Manual, if September 1 reservoir levels are less than 55 MAF, Gavins Point winter releases should be set at the minimum level of 12,000 cfs. If September 1 reservoir levels are greater than 58 MAF, Gavins Point releases should be set at 17,000 cfs.

and the Master Manual called for minimum winter releases of 12,000 cfs from Gavins Point. However, water intake owners in the lower basin were concerned about maintaining access to the river at those low flows, particularly since the 2011 flood scoured the river bottom in many areas. According to the Corps report describing reservoir management in 2012, the Corps exercised the flexibility in the Master Manual and elected to keep winter releases at 14,000 cfs to prevent municipalities and power plants from losing access to the river.

Drought conditions persisted into 2013, and the reservoir system was 7.4 MAF below the top of the Carryover Multiple Use zone on April 1. Due to the low volume of water in the reservoirs, the Corps continued implementing drought conservation measures, according to Corps officials. For example, navigation releases during April through June were at a minimum service level, meaning flows were high enough for an 8-foot-deep channel. The drought began to ease in parts of the basin during the summer due to rainfall and associated runoff. The higher volume of water in the reservoirs in July led to a slight increase in release rates for navigation, as well as a full 8-month navigation season. Runoff into the Missouri River reservoirs was about average in 2013 at 25.1 MAF, although water levels in the upper three reservoirs remained low.

Experts Agreed the Corps Made Appropriate Release Decisions during the Flood and Drought, under the Circumstances

Experts who participated in our meeting agreed that the Corps made appropriate release decisions during the flood and drought, given that neither the flood nor drought could have been predicted and the Corps' need to follow the guidelines in the Master Manual. These experts did not suggest changes to the Master Manual due to the 2011 flood or subsequent drought.

Experts Said the Corps Could Not Have Predicted or Prevented Flooding Due to Extreme Weather in 2011 and Its Release Decisions Were Appropriate

Experts who participated in our meeting discussed the above normal snowpack in the mountains and the plains, but they agreed the flood was triggered by the extreme rain in eastern Montana in May and June 2011. This conclusion is consistent with the December 2013 NOAA report examining climate extremes in the Missouri River basin that stated the record-setting rains were the final and, perhaps most critical, meteorological factor leading to high runoff and flooding in 2011. The experts agreed that no existing forecasting tools, including those used by the Corps and NOAA, could have accurately predicted the extreme rainstorms that occurred in Montana more than a week in advance. The December 2011 Independent Technical Review Panel Report commissioned by the Corps also reached this conclusion, noting that accurate prediction of precipitation more than a week in advance is beyond the current state of science.

Prior to our meeting, one of the experts reviewed information that was available on March 1, 2011, to determine what long-range forecast models were projecting about precipitation in the Missouri River basin for spring 2011. This expert noted that of the models he examined, only one forecasted a wet spring, and all other models forecasted normal or dry conditions. Based on the information the Corps had available in March 2011—these forecasts as well as evidence of the slightly above-normal mountain snowpack—experts who participated in our meeting said they considered the Corps release decisions early in the spring to be appropriate.

Experts who participated in our meeting also agreed that the Corps could not have prevented flooding in 2011. Snow continued to accumulate in the mountains in April and May—well past the average date of maximum snow accumulation. The experts said that, by June 2011, the volume of water coming into the reservoirs from the extreme rains and melting snow was so great that the Corps had no choice in June and July but to release water to accommodate the inflow and prevent damage to dam infrastructure, such as spillways in danger of being overtopped. The December 2011 Independent Technical Review Panel Report reached a similar conclusion. This report cited the absence of major dam failures as evidence of the Corps' success during the flood and noted that dam failure beginning at Fort Peck would have caused a catastrophic disaster of unprecedented magnitude.

Even if the Corps had decided on March 1, 2011, to increase releases due to the slightly larger-than-average snowpack in the mountains and plains, experts who participated in our meeting agreed that action would not have significantly reduced peak flows because of the extremely large amount of runoff in 2011. One of the experts said it would have taken several months for the Corps to release enough water from the reservoirs to make space for the runoff from the rainstorms and melting snow, and that action also could have resulted in downstream flooding. Specifically, this expert noted that high releases during the winter can cause flooding because of ice on the river, so the Corps would have needed to know in October 2010 about the upcoming extreme spring rain to release enough water in the fall to create more space in reservoirs.

One of the experts said that having additional space in the reservoirs on March 1 was the only way the Corps could have significantly reduced the peak downstream flooding. This expert also noted, however, that taking steps to lower reservoir levels in this way may not be consistent with the Master Manual. Another of the experts who participated in our meeting noted that while having more flood control storage available on March 1 each year reduces the chances of flooding, it could have negative effects on the other authorized purposes of the mainstem dams in nonflood years.

Experts Said the Corps Could Not Have Predicted the Drought in 2012 and Made Release Decisions in Accordance with the Master Manual

Experts who participated in our meeting generally agreed that the Missouri River basin's rapid descent into drought could not have been predicted. One of the experts qualified this statement, noting that the drought could not have been predicted with sufficient certainty to change reservoir decisions, given the high costs of the forecast being incorrect. Prior to the meeting, one of the experts reviewed information that was available in the spring of 2012 to determine what long-range forecast models were projecting about precipitation in the Missouri River basin for the remainder of 2012. This expert noted that there was no predictability; some of the models were forecasting wet conditions, and others were forecasting dry conditions. He also explained that some of the models predicting dry conditions frequently forecast dry conditions that do not materialize.

As the drought took hold, experts who participated in our meeting said the Corps followed procedures as laid out in the Master Manual. For example, the experts noted that, in 2012, the Corps released water for a full-service navigation season. The experts said that the navigation season was in accordance with the Master Manual, but it drained the reservoirs relatively quickly during the very dry summer of 2012. Specifically, according to the Corps report describing its management of the reservoir system in 2012, 22 percent of the water in storage was released in 2012, which would have reduced the amount of water available for future years if the drought lasted for several years.

Experts who participated in our meeting also agreed that the Corps appropriately exercised the reservoir release flexibility granted by the Master Manual. For example, the experts agreed it was appropriate that, in the winter of 2012-2013, the Corps kept winter releases higher than normal to ensure that water intakes along the river had continued access for municipal and industrial uses.

Experts Did Not Suggest Changes to the Master Manual

Experts who participated in our meeting agreed that the Corps does not need to change the Master Manual due to the 2011 flood or 2012 and 2013 drought, noting that there are no obvious deficiencies in the Master Manual. One of the experts noted that occurrence of similar extreme events should be incorporated in analyses that support any potential future changes in operating rules. In addition, several of the experts mentioned that developing the Master Manual took 17 years and that Missouri River basin stakeholders have agreed to the trade-offs and compromises in the current Master Manual. Other experts who participated in our meeting noted, however, that if the Corps could develop improved forecasting tools, it might be useful to evaluate whether changes to the Master Manual would help the Corps to act on information from the new tools. These experts explained that they were not sure whether such an evaluation would find that changes to the Master Manual would significantly help the Corps manage the reservoirs and balance the authorized purposes, but they thought it was worth examining if new forecasting tools are developed.

Finally, experts who participated in our meeting also discussed challenges the Corps faces in balancing reservoir releases for all eight authorized purposes. Some of the experts thought that the Corps should restart a study called the Missouri River Authorized Purposes Study (MRAPS). MRAPS was authorized in the Corps' fiscal year 2009 appropriations act to examine the extent to which the current authorized purposes of the river meet the needs of the residents of the Missouri River basin.[20] The Corps worked on MRAPS for 2 years before it was

---

[20] Energy and Water Development and Related Agencies Appropriations Act, 2009, Pub. L. No. 111-8, Division C, § 108, 123 Stat. 601, 607 (2009).

defunded by Congress in fiscal year 2011 appropriations.[21] Some of the experts thought that an examination of the purposes was warranted, in part, because of the number of reservoir regulation decisions made for the purpose of navigation. Another of the experts cautioned, however, that such a study might also open the idea of operating the Missouri River to benefit stakeholders outside the basin, such as navigators along the lower Mississippi River. This expert said that the navigation on the Mississippi River is a $1.2 billion industry and, in some years, could benefit from flow support from the Missouri River. He pointed out, however, that such an action could use a significant amount of water from the reservoirs, perhaps to the detriment of current authorized purposes. According to Corps officials, they are not authorized by Congress to make reservoir release decisions to support Mississippi River navigation.

Experts Identified Improvements in Data Collection and Forecasting That Could Help the Corps Make Better Release Decisions in Nonextreme Events

Experts who participated in our meeting suggested that collecting more hydrologic data, improving existing hydrologic data, and incorporating probabilistic forecasting techniques could improve the Corps' ability to make release decisions in nonextreme events. The experts stated that these data and forecasts would not have predicted the 2011 flood. However, they explained that these data and forecasts could be helpful in future, less extreme, floods.

Experts Said Improving Hydrologic Data Could Assist the Corps in Making Release Decisions

Experts who participated in our meeting suggested that improving existing hydrologic data and collecting new data could improve the Corps' ability to make release decisions. The experts mentioned that streamflow and precipitation data could be improved, and that new soil moisture, plains snowpack, and archaeological flood and drought data could be collected.[22] The experts said they did not believe that having these data

---

[21] Full-Year Continuing Appropriations Act, 2011, Pub. L. No. 112-10, Division B, § 1481, 125 Stat. 102, 131 (2011).

[22] In this section, archaeological data refers to paleoclimatic data, which is the study of weather and climate data from before human could make and record measurements. Paleoclimatologists can use this data to assemble thousands of years of climate history.

would have materially impacted the Corps' response to the 2011 flood. One of the experts said, while improved data would not have prevented the flood, it might have helped the Corps reduce the severity of the flood to a small degree. However, it is important to note that the hydrologic data systems discussed by the experts are not managed by the Corps but by other federal agencies as part of nationwide efforts to gather this data. Therefore, the Corps cannot directly control the extent to which improvements in these systems are made.

Streamflow Data

Experts who participated in our meeting said that maintaining and improving the USGS streamgage network is critical because it provides important data on current and historical streamflows. The experts said that historical streamflow records can also help modelers describe how flow conditions persist in streams, which enables them to create probabilistic forecasts of possible future river flows. As previously mentioned, USGS data indicates that about 9 percent of streamgages in the Missouri River basin have been discontinued in the last 10 years. USGS officials said that streamgages are often discontinued due to funding shortages, either at USGS or from the cooperative partner agencies which help fund the streamgages. According to USGS officials, the Corps provides funding for 264 of the 892 streamgages in the Missouri River basin. According to Corps officials, when their support for streamgages is reduced, they prioritize saving downstream streamgages on tributaries with more than one streamgage because downstream streamgages capture more of the river's flow. Corps officials said that under normal circumstances, losing data from upstream streamgages is not a serious problem, but that during a flood it can become a major challenge. For example, during the 2011 flood, the sole streamgage on the Judith River—a Missouri River tributary that runs through central Montana—was destroyed when the bridge it was attached to was washed away. Without streamflow data on the Judith River, the Corps had to estimate the Judith River flows, which resulted in less accurate information.

USGS officials said that they do their best to maintain the integrity of the streamgage network. USGS officials told us that most streamgages are funded through cooperation with federal, state and local government agencies. When streamgages are in danger of losing their funding, USGS officials work with their cooperative partners to find other funding sources to maintain the streamgage and are usually successful in finding funding for the most crucial ones. However, one of the experts who participated in our meeting said that the current cooperative funding model relied on by USGS to support most of the streamgages makes it a challenge to maintain the network since the cooperative partners may have other priorities. For example, USGS officials told us that one reservoir manager in Illinois pulled funding for a streamgage and used the money to build an outhouse. USGS officials began the National Streamflow Information Program in 2003 to federally fund a core network of 4,756 streamgages throughout the country. This program is designed to, among other things, improve USGS' ability to continue operating high-priority streamgages when partners discontinue funding. According to USGS officials, the National Streamflow Information Program received a $6 million funding increase in FY 2014 to $33 million.

Precipitation Data

Experts who participated in our meeting also identified gaps in the weather radar and precipitation gauge collection systems. Specifically, one of the experts said that weather radar does not do a good job of measuring winter precipitation and, even if it did, radar coverage in many parts of the basin is limited. For example, this expert noted that areas approximately 30 miles north of Pierre, South Dakota, have relatively poor radar coverage. Weather radar data is supplemented by precipitation gauge data, such as through the volunteer Community Collaborative Rain, Hail and Snow (CoCoRaHS) Network. However, the experts said that the basin is sparsely populated, which limits the pool of volunteer observers, potentially making it more difficult to collect the data needed to supplement the weather radar network. Corps officials said that the CoCoRaHS Network can compensate for gaps in the radar coverage, and few stakeholders are seeking to expand the radar network. NWS officials agreed that radar coverage was poor in the northern and western parts of the basin, such as southeastern Montana and central South Dakota. However, NWS officials told us that they do not currently have plans to expand radar coverage because current off-the-shelf radar does not have the same capabilities as the NWS's current system. Integrating off-the-shelf radars into the system would be difficult, and building radars that match the capabilities of the current system would be expensive, according to these officials. NWS officials said that new technology—such as the Multi-Radar Multi-Sensor system—will help mitigate the gaps in precipitation data in areas where radar coverage is sparse.

Soil Moisture and Snowpack Data

Experts who participated in our meeting said that making improvements to soil moisture and snowpack data would be very useful for making long-term forecasts because these conditions can be observed months before the associated runoff reaches the reservoir system. Some of the experts noted that there are major gaps in plains snowpack and soil moisture monitoring data, and improving these data would be useful in improving Corps' forecasting models. The experts said that gathering this data could be accomplished if the resources were available and stakeholders were willing to participate. A NOAA official working on the February 2013 interagency proposal to create a snowpack and soil moisture monitoring system said that NOAA is working with stakeholders to develop the interagency proposal, but implementation was on hold while stakeholders were waiting to see if it would be included in the then pending 2014 WRRDA.[23] However, this official noted that, even though the 2014 WRRDA requires the development of a monitoring system for soil moisture and snowpack data, there may be challenges in funding the proposal, which has a projected up-front cost of $6.25 million. Specifically, agencies supporting the proposal—such as the Corps, NOAA and NRCS—will need to find money for upfront costs in their existing budgets, which could take funds away from other programs and priorities. In addition, according to the February 2013 interagency proposal, maintaining the network once it is built would cost $1.46 million per year.

Archaeological Data

Some of the experts who participated in our meeting also recommended collecting archaeological data on floods and droughts, which could be used to provide a better understanding of the extreme floods and droughts in the basin before recordkeeping began in 1898. For example, USGS has ongoing archaeological work in the Black Hills of South Dakota that could allow a better understanding of how large a 10,000-year flood would be compared with a 100-year flood.[24] However, one of the experts cautioned that these data may not be useful for the Corps. According to a Corps official, these data would not be used in developing the manuals they use to guide regulation decisions, although it would provide information about the risk of larger floods.

---

[23] As previously discussed, this proposal would (1) enhance existing climate stations with snow depth and soil moisture sensors; (2) install new climate stations in the basin to enhance existing coverage; (3) enhance NOHRSC airborne surveys; (4) identify and train volunteer or part-time hires to conduct manual snow sampling; and (5) fund state coordinator positions in Montana, Nebraska, North Dakota, South Dakota, and Wyoming to coordinate snow surveys and other snow data networks at a state level.

[24] The "100-year flood" is a flood that has a 1 percent chance of occurring each year. This flood magnitude is used by federal agencies to administer floodplain management programs.

GAO-14-741 Missouri River Flood and Drought

Experts Identified Forecasting Techniques That Could Improve the Corps' Ability to Anticipate Weather Developments and Make Release Decisions

Experts who participated in our meeting agreed that by incorporating probabilistic techniques into runoff forecasts, the Corps could improve its ability to make release decisions in nonextreme events. Two of the experts indicated that probabilistic forecasting techniques could also improve the Corps' ability to make release decisions in extreme events. Experts who participated in our meeting agreed that probabilistic forecasting techniques could help the Corps manage risks and make decisions in the face of uncertainty. One of the experts said that these techniques are useful for communicating risk information—such as the risk of severe excesses or deficiencies of water—to the public and public officials. Another of the experts said that probabilistic techniques could allow the Corps to provide increased benefits to the system. These benefits could include higher reliability of water supply without increasing flood risk, increased flood protection, small increases in hydropower production, and easier implementation of variable river flows to create and maintain specific fish and wildlife habitats.

The primary type of probabilistic forecasting techniques discussed by experts who participated in our meeting was ensemble forecasting. Ensemble forecasting combines multiple forecasts to generate a sample of potential future weather developments. The individual forecasts, called ensemble members, can be created either using several different models in concert or multiple runs of the same model with slightly different initial conditions. These forecasts are then compared to determine how much agreement there is between the various ensemble members. Some of the experts said that ensemble forecasts can help forecasters correct for both uncertainty about initial conditions and uncertainty about the how a model is constructed, which are common causes of forecasting error.[25] One method of generating ensemble forecasts that the experts said could be potentially useful in the Missouri River basin is the Hirsch method.[26] This method uses correlations between 1 month's streamflow and the previous month's flow to generate ensemble members, since flow conditions from the previous month generally persist into the next. For example, Hirsch model forecasts examine the historical statistical relationships between

---

[25] Two experts said that ensemble forecasts can help forecasters understand the impact of uncertainty about initial conditions and model construction. One of these experts said that ensemble forecasts cannot correct or reduce uncertainty.

[26] This method is described in Robert M. Hirsch, "Stochastic Hydrologic Model for Drought Management." *Journal of the Water Resources Planning and Management Division,* vol. 107, no. 2 (October 1981): 303-313.

streamflow in March and streamflow in April since March's conditions persist into April. When this relationship exists, it allows for forecasts with less variance and uncertainty compared with other methods, leading to more accurate forecasts.

Another way experts who participated in our meeting suggested that the Corps could incorporate ensemble modeling into its forecasts would be to leverage the existing ensemble streamflow forecast created by the NWS Advanced Hydrologic Prediction Service (AHPS). The AHPS forecasts use ensemble streamflow predictions to determine the chances of a river exceeding minor, moderate, or major flood levels over the next 90 days. One of the experts noted that the current AHPS forecast locations in the Missouri River basin are not located where the Corps likely needs them to be to have enough information to make their decisions. NWS officials told us that they produce probabilistic forecasts at 465 AHPS forecast locations in the basin but that none of these locations are along the mainstem of the Missouri River because probabilistic forecasting along the mainstem would require integrating the Corps' reservoir management procedures into the NWS probabilistic models. One of the experts said the Corps could overcome this challenge by identifying statistical relationships between the existing AHPS locations and the locations that the Corps would want to use for decision making and conduct a pilot project to see how useful these statistical relationships would be for reservoir management decisions. This expert said that this pilot effort would not be a difficult undertaking and could be accomplished for roughly $100,000, but the Corps would need to coordinate closely with NWS.

According to experts who participated in our meeting, reservoir managers in several basins throughout the United States currently use probabilistic techniques to manage reservoirs. For example, reservoir managers in the Occoquan River basin (which provides drinking water to Fairfax County, Virginia) successfully used Hirsch method forecasts in the 1970s to support implementation of drought mitigation measures that were less onerous than were thought necessary based on their deterministic forecasts. In 2009, the New York City Department of Environmental Protection (DEP) began developing a tool that incorporates both Hirsch method and NWS forecasts to help manage drinking water reservoirs that serve 9 million residents of the city and surrounding areas, as well as other competing demands on the system, such as release requirements on the Delaware River, flood control, and recreational fisheries. DEP officials said that a similar tool could help the Corps better manage other reservoir systems, such as along the Missouri River. DEP officials said

New York City Reservoir System

Drinking water for New York City comes from 6 reservoirs in the Delaware-Catskill River basin, located west of the Hudson River, and from 12 reservoirs and three controlled lakes east of the Hudson. Ninety percent of the city's water comes from the 6 Delaware-Catskills reservoirs. Water from these reservoirs reaches the city by several aqueducts. Total storage capacity in these reservoirs is 550 billion gallons, or 1.69 million acre-feet.

Source: GAO. | GAO-14-741

the tool, which cost about $8 million, was developed in stages: in late 2010, it included modeling based on the Hirsch method and, in November 2013 it incorporated NWS hydrologic ensemble forecasts.[27] DEP officials said the tool uses these ensemble forecasts to model potential reservoir management scenarios to meet water quality goals—such as reducing the amount of sediment in the city's drinking water—without having to install expensive new water filtration plants. DEP officials also said the tool supports reservoir operations decisions, including preemptive releases in advance of large storm events to create space in the reservoirs and releases to support downstream communities. DEP officials said the tool is more effective than their previous method of forecasting, which, much like the Corps' Missouri River forecasting, used historical data and runoff volume calculations. DEP officials said that ensemble forecasts have been effective in modernizing management of their reservoir system by reducing uncertainty and helping them to better assess risk and make informed decisions, and that similar systems could help the Corps make risk-based decisions about reservoir releases informed by real probabilities.

Corps officials told us that they have not considered using probabilistic techniques, such as the Hirsch method or NWS forecast products, in the Missouri River system because they are not sure the benefits would outweigh the difficulty of creating the models or explaining the new methods to their stakeholders. Corps officials told us that deterministic forecasts are easy to maintain and simpler to explain to stakeholders than probabilistic methods. These officials also said that their current methods work well in all but the most extreme events and are a more efficient use of their limited staff resources. Corps officials said that assigning probabilities to their current runoff forecast could give them and their stakeholders more certainty about the likelihood that a very high or very low runoff year will develop. However, the Corps would nonetheless have to select one of the forecasts on which to base their real-time operations. This would, in effect, require the application of the same engineering judgment that is used in their deterministic forecast, according to Corps officials. In addition, Corps officials said that Missouri River basin stakeholders who see the results of the Corps models would face similar

---

[27] Specifically, the DEP tool uses forecasts from AHPS and the NWS's new Hydrologic Ensemble Forecast Service, which provides information based on current conditions, weather forecasts, and longer-term climate forecasts. DEP officials said that the HEFS weather forecast goes out about 15 days

challenges, but they would not have the years of engineering expertise to determine how to act on a range of potential very high or very low releases with the same likelihood of occurrence. Furthermore, Corps officials said that basing system operations on probabilistic forecasts would require changes to many of their current operational procedures, and thus changes to the Master Manual.

However, experts who participated in our meeting agreed that Corps should investigate probabilistic techniques. Some of the experts said that the Corps can achieve better outcomes for the basin using probabilistic techniques than their current methods. One of the experts noted that using probabilistic techniques can help the Corps focus on the risks of flood and drought in less extreme years than 2011, which may help to increase the benefits to basin stakeholders from the six mainstem dams. The experts also agreed on the importance of evaluating any new forecasting methods using hindcasting, which uses historical weather and stream information to determine how effectively a given forecasting approach would have predicted past events. One of the experts said that hindcasts are a powerful tool for showing the Corps and their stakeholders that a new probabilistic forecasting model would have provided useful information in the past, will be able to provide useful information in the future, and that changes to operating rules based on the ensemble forecasts would create win-win outcomes.

Stakeholders Were Generally Satisfied with Corps' Communication during the Flood and Drought

During both the 2011 flood and the subsequent drought, the Corps communicated with Missouri River stakeholders in a variety of ways, which most stakeholders we interviewed said were effective.[28] Nearly all stakeholders we interviewed were generally satisfied with the Corps' communication with them during these events, saying that the information they received from the Corps was timely and sufficient for their purposes.

---

[28] In this section of the report, we defined "nearly all" as 85 percent of stakeholders who answered a given question; "most" as more than 50 percent, but less than 85 percent; "some" as more than 30 percent, but less than 50 percent; "several" as more than 15 percent, but less than 30 percent; and "a few" as less than 15 percent.

Stakeholders Received Information from the Corps in a Variety of Ways and Most Said Methods Were Effective

Stakeholders we interviewed said that the Corps communicated with them in a variety of ways during both the flood and drought. For most stakeholders, the Corps was the primary source of information during the flood, but fewer than half of these stakeholders used the Corps as their primary source of information during the drought.[29] In both events, most stakeholders said that the methods through which they received information from the Corps were the most effective way for the Corps to communicate with them.[30]

As shown in table 3, many of the communication methods mentioned by the stakeholders we interviewed were used by the Corps in both the flood and drought. One of those methods was the Corps' conference calls. According to Corps officials, these calls began in May 2011 as a way to provide daily updates and information during the flood to congressional representatives, state and local officials, and the news media about (1) planned water releases from the six Corps dams on the Missouri River, (2) weather forecasts, and (3) the Corps' repair schedule. The conference calls also gave these stakeholders an opportunity to ask the Corps questions about their own communities. In 2012 and 2013, the Corps continued these calls on an almost monthly basis during the winter and spring runoff season. Nearly all of the stakeholders we interviewed reported that they took part in the conference calls at some point. Stakeholders also reported receiving information from the Corps via e-mail. For example, a few stakeholders mentioned receiving information during the flood in e-mails from a Corps district official who updated them on release rates and provided other useful information. One of these stakeholders reported that, if they had questions, they could contact this official by e-mail and would obtain a response. During the drought, one stakeholder said that he received monthly updates about the reservoir by e-mail. In addition, some stakeholders mentioned communication methods specific to the drought. For example, four stakeholders mentioned receiving a letter from the Corps that was sent to water intake owners in April 2013 warning of a potential need to reduce water releases from Gavins Point dam to as low as 9,000 cfs in the fall of 2013 as a

---

[29] We conducted interviews with a total of 45 stakeholders. However, because not all stakeholders responded to each question, the total number of responses varies for each question.

[30] Thirty-four of 41 reported the methods were effective during the flood; 24 of 27 reported the methods were effective during the drought.

GAO-14-741 Missouri River Flood and Drought

conservation measure.[31] This letter asked water intake owners to take steps to ensure that their intakes would operate at the low levels.

Table 3: U.S. Army Corps of Engineers' Communication Methods That Stakeholders Reported

	Flood	Drought
Corps conference call	X	X
E-mail	X	X
Individual conversation with local Corps officials	X	X
Press releases	X	X
Direct telephone call	X	X
Corps website	X	X
Technical assistance in emergency operations center	X	
Social media	X	
Annual Operating Plan public meetings	X	X
April 2013 Corps letter related to Gavins Point dam		X
Missouri River Recovery Implementation Committee [a]	X	X
Other Corps-sponsored public meetings	X	X
Press conferences	X	
Silver Jackets Program [b]		X

Source: GAO. | GAO-14-741

[a]The Missouri River Recovery Implementation Committee is a basin-wide collaborative forum to provide guidance on implementation of ecosystem restoration measures.

[b]The Silver Jackets Program, supported by the National Flood Risk Management Program, provides an opportunity to improve collaboration between state, federal, and tr bal and local agencies.

Most of the stakeholders we interviewed said they were satisfied with the amount of input they had on how the Corps manages the river during drought. Most of the stakeholders also said that they commented on the Corps' draft Annual Operating Plan, which describes the Corps' plans for managing the river for that year. However, seven stakeholders said that the Corps solicits their input but does not do anything with it.

---

[31] The Corps did not lower releases to that level in fall 2013. Normal fall/winter releases from Gavins Point dam during a drought are between 12,000-14,000 cfs. According to the Corps' April 2013 letter, lowering releases to 9,000 cfs could result in water intakes not being able to reach the river, even if there was enough water in the river to meet all water supply needs.

In addition to the information provided by the Corps, nearly all of the stakeholders we interviewed reported receiving information from sources other than the Corps during both the flood and drought. These other sources of information included state agencies; federal agencies such as USGS, NWS, and NOAA; news media; and local officials.[32] These sources provided different kinds of data, which stakeholders said they used in addition to the information they received from the Corps to respond to the flood and the drought. Other sources of information were mostly similar during the flood and the drought. However, several stakeholders said that they used the U.S. Drought Monitor during the drought.[33]

Nearly All Stakeholders Were Generally Satisfied with the Corps' Communication during the Flood

Nearly all of the stakeholders we interviewed were generally satisfied with the Corps' communication during the flood. The information they received from the Corps helped them take a number of actions, as shown in table 4. For example, officials from several state and local governments agencies said they used information from the Corps to identify infrastructure that would be affected by floodwaters and either protect it by sandbagging or, if possible, relocate it out of the flood zone. Other stakeholders, such as one state parks department official, used the Corps' information to plan for facility closures or remove equipment to prevent damage. Stakeholders also shared information they received from the Corps with other people. For example, one state agency official shared the Corps information with others in his agency, with other state agencies, and with farmers and levee districts throughout the state. Similarly, one nonprofit organization official disseminated information to its members who are located throughout the Missouri River basin.

---

[32] NWS is an agency within NOAA. However, other agencies and centers within NOAA provide information to stakeholders, such as the National Climatic Data Center.

[33] In addition to these sources, a few stakeholders also said that they received information during both the flood and the drought from sources, such as the U.S. Bureau of Reclamation, the U.S. Forest Service, or personal observations.

Table 4: How Stakeholders Reported Using Information Received from the U.S. Army Corps of Engineers during the Flood of 2011

How stakeholders used Corps information	Number of stakeholders[a]
Inform organization's flood preparations	23
Sharing information	20
Protecting infrastructure	16
Staying informed	9
Assist others with flood preparations	5
Inform requests for studies of flood impact on fish and wildlife	4
Other[b]	3

Source: GAO. | GAO-14-741

[a]Forty-two stakeholders responded to this question. Numbers total more than 42 because some stakeholders reported using the information for more than one purpose.

[b]Other ways that stakeholders reported using information received from the Corps in the flood of 2011 included assisting others with post-flood recovery, writing articles in the news media, and assisting in inundation mapping efforts.

Most of the stakeholders we interviewed said that the information they received from the Corps was sufficient for their purposes. For example, one state agency official praised the inundation maps received from the Corps for having considerable amounts of useful information, and also praised the Corps' status updates about which levees were in danger of failing or had already failed due to the effects of the flood.[34] In contrast, several stakeholders said that the information was not sufficient for their purposes. For example, 8 stakeholders said that the Corps changed their water release estimates from the dams too frequently. Specifically, one stakeholder reported that during May 2011, the Corps revised its release estimates upward five times in a 2-week span. The final estimate, provided in early June, was nearly three times the size of the first estimate from mid-May. This stakeholder said his agency had to revise flood control plans after each estimate, and that his agency eventually decided to plan for the highest possible releases rather than frequently revising its plans.

Most of the stakeholders we interviewed said that the Corps' information was generally timely. For example, one state agency official said that the

---

[34] Inundation maps are a series of maps that depict which areas are likely to flood at specific river levels.

Corps provided data in a timely manner, and that the agency was always informed when the Corps planned to increase releases and by how much. Similarly, a local government official said that while he did not always like what the Corps was telling him, the Corps always provided accurate and timely data about when the releases were going to change, and by how much. In contrast, 5 stakeholders said that the Corps information was generally untimely during the flood, and 5 others said that the Corps' information was untimely in the beginning stages of the flood but improved over time. Seven of the 10 stakeholders who cited problems with timeliness were located in North and South Dakota, the states where five of the six Corps dams are located.[35]

Although nearly all of the stakeholders we interviewed were satisfied with the Corps' communication during the flood, most stakeholders offered at least one suggestion for how the Corps could improve its communication during future floods. However, there was no consensus among stakeholders on these suggestions. A few stakeholders suggested that the Corps communicate any uncertainty associated with its release estimates. One of these stakeholders explained that this could include the Corps telling them the worst-case scenario for releases, not just the most likely case. Corps officials expressed concerns about communicating this type of information with their release estimates since it could be difficult to use without the appropriate context. In addition, a few stakeholders suggested that the Corps hold a conference call specifically for agency officials. One of these stakeholders said that having the news media on the call made it difficult to discuss sensitive response-related information. Corps officials also said that having separate conference calls for agency officials and elected officials and media is feasible and that they would consider this in the future. In contrast, some stakeholders said there is nothing more the Corps could do to improve communication in the event of another flood. A few stakeholders identified actions the Corps took during the flood that they appreciated such as having a Corps official embedded in their emergency operations center.

---

[35] One stakeholder indicated that the information was untimely, but said that it was the fault of state officials getting information to him, not the Corps.

Nearly All Stakeholders Were Generally Satisfied with Corps' Communication during the Drought

Nearly all of the stakeholders we interviewed who were in contact with the Corps were generally satisfied with the Corps' communication during the drought. These stakeholders used the information they received to take a number of actions, as shown in table 5. For example, officials from one local government used the information they received from the Corps to analyze options to update their intake to ensure that it would remain operational if the Corps' winter releases dropped to 9,000 cfs. As was the case during the flood, some of these stakeholders said that they shared information with others during the drought. For example, one nonprofit official said that he disseminated Corps information to Missouri River navigators, shipping companies, and agricultural producers, among others. Nearly all of these stakeholders said that the Corps gave them sufficient information for their purposes. One state agency official said that he had a "good handle" on the problems caused by drought and that the Corps has explained things well.

Table 5: How Stakeholders Reported Using Information Received from the U.S. Army Corps of Engineers during the Drought of 2012 and 2013

How stakeholders used Corps information	Number of stakeholders[a]
Manage drought preparations	13
Sharing information	9
Staying informed	5
Assisting others with drought preparations	2
Fish and wildlife monitoring	1
Other[b]	2

Source: GAO. | GAO-14-741

[a]Twenty-seven stakeholders responded to this question. Numbers total more than 27 because some stakeholders reported using the information for more than one purpose.

[b]Other ways that stakeholders reported using information received from the Corps in the drought of 2012 and 2013 included suggesting alternatives to the Corps' proposed operations and advocating for reservoir operations that would help fish spawning in reservoirs.

Nearly all of the stakeholders we interviewed said that the Corps communicated with them in a timely fashion. However, 8 of these stakeholders said that the issue of timeliness is different in a drought than during a flood. As one stakeholder explained, droughts do not present the same type of near-term safety issues that must be dealt with immediately. Instead, droughts stress the water system at a lower level over a longer period of time. Although nearly all of the stakeholders we interviewed were satisfied with the Corps' communication during the drought, some stakeholders offered suggestions for how the Corps could improve its communication during future droughts. However, there was no consensus among stakeholders on these suggestions. The most common suggestion, mentioned by several stakeholders was that the Corps make better use of technology in presenting information, such as by improving their website. Corps officials acknowledged the importance of a user friendly website and that it can be hard to find information on their current website. These officials noted that redesigning a website would take a significant effort and that doing so is not a high priority given current staffing and funding levels. However, these officials mentioned that some website improvements have been made recently, such as adding a map of streamgages within the basin with links to the raw data, which could be on Corps, U.S. Bureau of Reclamation, USGS, or NWS websites. Most stakeholders did not have suggestions for the Corps on improving communication in future droughts.

Conclusions

The extreme flood of 2011 followed by severe drought in 2012 and 2013 created challenging conditions on the Missouri River for the Corps. Experts who participated in our meeting agreed that the Corps made appropriate release decisions during the flood and drought, given the circumstances. However, the experts agreed that techniques such as probabilistic forecasting have the potential to improve the Corps' ability to make release decisions in nonextreme events. Probabilistic forecasting could allow the Corps to make better risk-based decisions and provide increased benefits to residents in the Missouri River basin, such as higher reliability of water supply, increased flood protection, small increases in hydropower production, and easier implementation of variable river flows to create fish and wildlife habitats. However, the Corps currently uses deterministic forecasting methods, and Corps officials told us that they have not assessed the pros and cons of using probabilistic techniques because they are not sure that the benefits of more sophisticated probabilistic modeling techniques would outweigh the difficulty of creating the models or explaining the new methods to the stakeholders in the Missouri River basin. New forecasting methods can be evaluated—using a technique known as hindcasting—to determine how effectively a new forecasting approach would have predicted past events. According to the experts, hindcasting is a powerful tool for showing the Corps and their stakeholders that a new probabilistic forecasting model would have provided useful information in the past, will be able to provide useful information in the future, and that changes to operating rules based on the ensemble forecasts would create win-win outcomes.

Recommendation for Executive Action

To ensure the U.S. Army Corps of Engineers considers a full range of forecasting options to manage the Missouri River mainstem reservoir system, we recommend that the Secretary of Defense direct the Secretary of the Army to direct the Chief of Engineers and Commanding General of the U.S. Army Corps of Engineers to evaluate the pros and cons of probabilistic forecasting techniques that could improve the U.S. Army Corps of Engineers' ability to anticipate weather developments, and to evaluate whether forecasting changes are warranted.

Agency Comments

We provided a draft of this product to the Departments of Commerce, Defense, and the Interior for comment. In its written comments, reprinted in appendix III, the Department of Defense concurred with our recommendation and noted that it will take steps to address the recommendation. The Department of Commerce provided technical comments that we incorporated as appropriate. The Department of the Interior had no comments.

We are sending copies of this report to the appropriate congressional committees; the Secretaries of Commerce, Defense, and the Interior; and other interested parties. In addition, the report is available at no charge on the GAO website at http://www.gao.gov.

If you or your staff have any questions about this report, please contact me at (202) 512-3841 or fennella@gao.gov. Contact points for our Offices of Congressional Relations and Public Affairs may be found on the last page of this report. GAO staff who made key contributions to this report are listed in appendix IV.

Anne-Marie Fennell
Director,
Natural Resources and Environment

List of Requesters

The Honorable John Hoeven
Ranking Member
Subcommittee on the Legislative Branch
Committee on Appropriations
United States Senate

The Honorable Roy Blunt
United States Senate

The Honorable Chuck Grassley
United States Senate

The Honorable Tom Harkin
United States Senate

The Honorable Heidi Heitkamp
United States Senate

The Honorable Mike Johanns
United States Senate

The Honorable Timothy Johnson
United States Senate

The Honorable Claire McCaskill
United States Senate

The Honorable Jerry Moran
United States Senate

The Honorable Pat Roberts
United States Senate

The Honorable Jon Tester
United States Senate

The Honorable John Thune
United States Senate

Appendix I: List of Experts and Discussion Questions

Experts

Larry Cieslik, retired, U.S. Army Corps of Engineers (Corps)

David Ford, David Ford Consulting Engineers

Terry Fulp, U.S. Bureau of Reclamation

Bob Hirsch, U.S. Geological Survey

David Maidment, University of Texas

John Schaake, retired, National Weather Service

Dan Sheer, Hydrologics

Dennis Todey, South Dakota State University

Eric Wood, Princeton University

Discussion Questions

- Does the Corps have access to adequate data and forecasting information that allows them to make timely release decisions during droughts and floods? If not, why? What are the consequences of not having this data and forecasting?

- If data elements needed for decision making are missing, what technical challenges, if any, are there in collecting these data?

- Based on information presented by the Corps about how they use data collected by federal and state agencies, are those data being used to support reservoir operations decisions, as appropriate? Why, or why not?

- How should the Corps make reservoir operations decisions in the face of uncertainty in runoff forecasts? How, if at all, should the Corps incorporate uncertainty in runoff forecasts into information provided to basin stakeholders or the public?

- What are the pros and cons of the Corps' policy to regulate releases based on "water on the ground"?

- What steps, if any, could the Corps take to improve runoff forecasting?

- In the 2011 flood, were there additional reservoir release actions the Corps might have taken to better manage flood risks and, if so, what may have been the consequences of not taking these actions? What constraints might exist on those actions?

- In the 2012 and 2013 drought, were there additional reservoir release actions the Corps might have taken to better manage drought risk and, if so, what may have been the consequences of not taking these actions? What constraints might exist on those actions?

- Does the Corps have appropriate flexibility to regulate the river to manage risk of flood and drought? What are the pros and cons of the current amount of flexibility the Corps has?

- During low water conditions, the Corps works to balance the competing interests of the eight authorized purposes of the Missouri River reservoirs. How well is the Corps balancing these purposes and what, if any, improvements could the Corps make? What constraints might exist on those actions?

- The most recent changes to the Master Manual raise the threshold below which the Corps regulates the system in drought conservation mode. What are the pros, and cons, of this new threshold?

Appendix II: Objectives, Scope, and Methodology

This report describes (1) experts' views on the Corps' release decisions during the 2011 flood and 2012 and 2013 drought; (2) additional actions, if any, experts recommend to improve the Corps' ability to make future release decisions; and (3) stakeholders' views on how the Corps communicated information during the flood and drought and improvements, if any, stakeholders suggest.

To address all of our objectives, we reviewed relevant laws, including the Flood Control Act of 1944 that authorized the construction of dams along the Missouri River. In addition, we reviewed the documents that the U.S. Army Corps of Engineers (Corps) uses to guide their release decisions, including the Missouri River Mainstem Reservoir System Master Water Control Manual (Master Manual) (last updated in 2006) and the Annual Operating Plans for 2010-2011, 2011-2012, and 2012-2013. We also reviewed documents produced or commissioned by the Corps that describe the details of the Corps' release decisions during the flood and drought, including "Summary of Actual 2011 Regulation," "Summary of Actual 2012 Regulation," and the December 2011 Independent Technical Review Report. In addition, we reviewed National Oceanic and Atmospheric Administration (NOAA) and U.S. Geological Survey (USGS) documents about existing hydrologic data collection systems and National Weather Service (NWS) documents about weather and flood forecasts during 2011. We conducted a technical review of the December 2011 Independent Technical Review Report and the NOAA Climate Assessment Report to ensure that the methodologies used were appropriate to support the conclusions reached. We also interviewed Corps officials at the Missouri River Basin Water Management Division who are responsible for making release decisions and conducted a site visit to the Oahe project in South Dakota to gather information about dam operations and water levels during the 2011 flood.

To obtain expert views on the Corps' information and release decisions, we convened a meeting of experts to discuss these issues. This meeting was held at the National Academy of Sciences (NAS) in February 2014, and staff at NAS assisted in identifying experts for the meeting. To identify the experts appropriate for this meeting, NAS staff solicited nominations from: current and former members of the NAS Water Science and Technology Board; current and former members of the Water Science and Technology Board study committees; select members of the NAS and the National Academy of Engineering; National Research Council staff; and other experts. Experts were selected based on knowledge of: (1) reservoir operations and river basin system modeling (both in the United States and abroad); (2) weather conditions and

forecasts, and river stage forecasting, specifically in the Missouri River
system; and (3) modeling of the relationship between precipitation and
runoff; and Corps operational decisions. The experts identified by NAS
included individuals with a broad set of viewpoints and knowledge,
including experts from federal and state government agencies, the private
sector and consultants, academia, and retired federal water and
engineering experts. The range of the experts' expertise included
reservoir system operations and modeling, hydrology and hydraulics, civil
engineering, meteorology, rainfall-runoff modeling, and Corps reservoir
operations.

The nine experts were evaluated for conflicts of interest. A conflict of
interest was considered to be any current financial or other interest that
might conflict with the service of an individual because it (1) could impair
objectivity and (2) could create an unfair competitive advantage for any
person or organization. All potential conflicts were discussed by NAS and
GAO staff. The nine experts were determined to be free of conflicts of
interest, and the group as a whole was judged to have no inappropriate
biases. See appendix I for a list of the experts and the questions
discussed during the 2-day meeting.

The 2-day expert meeting began with a 1-hour presentation by the Chief
of the Missouri River Basin Water Management Division and an
opportunity for the experts to ask questions. After questions, the Corps'
representative left the meeting and experts began discussing the Corps'
data, forecasts, and release decisions. The meeting was recorded and
transcribed to ensure that we accurately captured the experts'
statements, and we reviewed the transcripts as a source of evidence. We
analyzed the transcripts to identify key statements the experts made
regarding the Corps' data, forecasts, and release decisions. We sent
these statements, via e-mail, to each of the experts to ensure that they all
agreed with our characterization of the findings of the 2-day meeting. We
received replies from all nine experts generally agreeing to the
statements and making some additions and clarifications, which we
incorporated as appropriate.

To obtain stakeholders' views of the Corps' communication during flood
and drought, we used a standard set of questions to interview a
nonprobability sample of 45 stakeholders in the Missouri River basin. We
identified these stakeholders based on our preliminary interviews and
sought to include organizations from each of the seven states included in
our review and related to the eight authorized purposes of the Missouri
River reservoir system. For example, to obtain perspectives related to

flood control, we identified communities of different sizes along the river and interviewed officials from those communities responsible for emergency management and public works. These local communities included cities as large as Kansas City, Missouri (more than 450,000 people), and as small as Fort Pierre, South Dakota (roughly 2,000 people). We also spoke with state emergency management agencies in each of the seven states. Similarly, to obtain perspectives related to navigation, we interviewed a barge operator, a terminal operator, and nonprofit organizations that advocate for navigation along the Missouri River. In addition, to obtain perspectives related to fish and wildlife, we interviewed an official at the U.S. Fish and Wildlife Service active in addressing endangered species in the Missouri River basin and state officials involved in fish and wildlife issues from each of the seven states. See table 6 for a complete list of the stakeholders we interviewed about the Corps' communication efforts.

Table 6: Stakeholders Interviewed

Montana	Department of Disaster and Emergency Services
	Department of Fish Wildlife and Parks
	Department of Natural Resources and Conservation
	Missouri River Conservation Districts Council
North Dakota	Department of Game and Fish
	Department of Homeland Security
	Department of Parks and Recreation
	Bismarck Emergency Management Division
	Bismarck Department of Public Works
	Friends of Lake Sakakawea
South Dakota	Department of Game, Fish and Parks
	Department of Environment and Natural Resources
	Department of Public Safety
	Fort Pierre Department of Public Works
	Yankton Water Department
Kansas	Department of Wildlife Parks and Tourism
	Division of Emergency Management
	Leavenworth Department of Public Works
	Leavenworth County Office of Emergency Management
	Leavenworth Water Department
Nebraska	Emergency Management Agency
	Game and Parks Commission
	Plattsmouth Office of the City Administrator
	Blair Department of Public Works

Iowa	Department of Agriculture and Land Stewardship
	Department of Homeland Security and Emergency Management
	Department of Natural Resources
	Tegra Corporation
	Sioux City Fire Rescue
	Woodbury County Department of Disaster and Emergency Services
Missouri	Department of Conservation
	Department of Natural Resources
	State Emergency Management Agency
	Kansas City Office of Emergency Management
	Kansas City Power and Light
	Kansas City Board of Public Utilities
	Hermann Sand and Gravel
No specific state	Missouri River Association of States and Tribes
	Missouri and Associated Rivers Coalition
	Coalition to Protect the Missouri River
	Izaak Walton League
	Healthy Rivers Partnership
	U.S. Fish and Wildlife Service
	Western Area Power Administration
	Rosebud Sioux Tribe

Source: GAO. | GAO-14-741

To obtain the views of these 45 agencies and organizations, we
developed a structured interview guide that included questions about the
Corps' mode of communication with stakeholders (for example, via e-
mail, phone, or letter), and how effective that communication was during
the recent flood and drought. We conducted two pretests of the
questionnaire and made appropriate changes based on these pretests.
We used the structured interview guide to obtain the views of these
organizations either via phone or, in cases where the respondent
preferred, via e-mail. We analyzed the responses to provide insight into
organizations' views on the Corps' communication during the flood and
drought. These stakeholder interviews provide key insights and illustrate
opinions concerning Missouri River basin issues; however the results of
our interviews cannot be used to make generalizations about all views. In
some cases, interview questions were skipped, as appropriate. For
example, some stakeholders did not interact with the Corps during the
drought, and we did not ask these stakeholders questions about the
Corps' communication during that time.

We conducted this performance audit from August 2012 to September
2014 in accordance with generally accepted government auditing

standards. Those standards require that we plan and perform the audit to
obtain sufficient, appropriate evidence to provide a reasonable basis for
our findings and conclusions based on our audit objectives. We believe
that the evidence obtained provides a reasonable basis for our findings
and conclusions based on our audit objectives.

Appendix III: Comments from the Department of Defense

DEPARTMENT OF THE ARMY
OFFICE OF THE ASSISTANT SECRETARY
CIVIL WORKS
108 ARMY PENTAGON
WASHINGTON DC 20310-0108

AUG 1 8 2014

Ms. Anne-Marie Fennell
Director, Natural Resources and Environment
U.S. Government Accountability Office
441 G Street, NW
Washington, D.C. 20548

Dear Ms. Fennell:

Enclosed is the Department of Defense response to the U.S. Government Accountability Office Draft Report GAO-14-741, "MISSOURI RIVER FLOOD AND DROUGHT Experts Agree the Corps Took Appropriate Action, Given the Circumstances, but Should Examine New Forecasting Techniques," dated September 2014 (GAO Code 361435).

The Department concurs with the recommendation of the report and will seek appropriate resources to initiate an evaluation of probabilistic forecasting techniques. The evaluation will assess the pros and cons of these forecasting techniques for potential integration into the U.S. Army Corps of Engineers decision-making processes.

The Department is providing official written comments for inclusion in the report.

Very truly yours,

Jo-Ellen Darcy
Assistant Secretary of the Army
(Civil Works)

Enclosure

Printed on   Recycled Paper

GAO Draft Report Dated July 25, 2014
GAO-14-741 (GAO Code 361435)

"MISSOURI RIVER FLOOD AND DROUGHT Experts Agree the Corps Took
Appropriate Action, Given the Circumstances, but Should Examine New
Forecasting Techniques"

DEPARTMENT OF DEFENSE COMMENTS
TO THE GAO RECOMMENDATION

RECOMMENDATION: The GAO recommends that the Secretary of Defense direct the
Secretary of the Army to direct the Chief of Engineers and Commanding General of the
U.S. Army Corps of Engineers to evaluate the pros and cons of probabilistic forecasting
techniques that could improve the U.S. Army Corps of Engineers' ability to anticipate
weather developments, and to evaluate whether forecasting changes are warranted.

DEPARTMENT OF DEFENSE RESPONSE: The Department of Defense concurs with
the recommendation. The U.S. Army Corps of Engineers will initiate an evaluation of
probabilistic forecasting techniques, subject to the availability of funds for this
evaluation. The evaluation will assess the pros and cons of these forecasting
techniques for potential integration into the Corps decision making processes. Once
resources have been provided, it is estimated that the evaluation could be completed
within 18 months in coordination with appropriate agencies.

Appendix IV: GAO Contact and Staff Acknowledgments

GAO Contact	Anne-Marie Fennell, (202) 512-3841 or fennella@gao.gov
Staff Acknowledgments	In addition to the individual named above, Vondalee R. Hunt (Assistant Director); Cheryl Arvidson; Elizabeth Beardsley; Michelle Cooper; Cindy Gilbert; Geoffrey Hamilton; Armetha Liles; Perry Lusk, Jr.; and Janice Poling made key contributions to this report.